The Bandit Wind

The Bandit Wind

Poems by Slavko Janevski
Translations by Charles Simic

THE STRUGA SERIES OF MACEDONIAN POETS
Milne Holton, General Editor

 DRYAD PRESS
Takoma Park, Maryland

Acknowledgements

A number of these translations first appeared in *Delos*, published at
the University of Maryland. Special thanks to Mark Esterman, Sandy
Harpe and Ronna Hammer.

Published in the United States by
Dryad Press
15 Sherman Avenue, Takoma Park, Maryland 20912

Library of Congress Cataloging in Publication Data
Janevski, Slavko
      Poems.   English and Macedonian.   Selections
      The bandit wind: poems/by Slavko Janevski
      translated by Charles Simic.—Washington, D.C.: Dryad Press, 1989
            p.   cm.—(The Struga series of Macedonian poetry)
      Poems in Macedonian and English
      ISBN: 0-931848-76-8 — ISBN 0-931848-77-6 (pbk.)

      1. Janevski, Slavko—Translations, English. I.Title.II.Series
PG1195.J3A27 891.8′191 — c190   89-1176

Contents

I

II

III

Contents

Introduction

History, it is said, is shaped by geography, and certainly poetry is shaped by history. Macedonia, that great bowl full of the most fertile of Balkan earth, tilted south toward the Aegean Sea, can hold no exception to these rules. Like Ireland, its rich central valley is ringed by mountains—the Pirin to the east toward Bulgaria, the Serbian highlands to the north, Albania's highlands to the west. And all these mountains are pierced by many passes for travelers and merchants and soldiers to pour through.

This rich prize of fertile land has been populated since neolithic times. A monarchic state emerged there in the 4th century, B.C., under a king named Philip and his son Alexander; for a short time that monarchy would dominate the known world. But the Slavic peoples, to whom modern Macedonians trace their origins, did not appear in the area in significant numbers until the seventh century A.D., a thousand years later, at a time when the region was dominated by the Byzantine emperors. These Slavs were rather immediately Christianized by the Byzantines and remained under Christian rulers until the fourteenth century, when Ottoman Turks overran both the Balkans and Byzantium and held sway for five hundred years.

The still Orthodox Christian Slavs of Macedonia remained relatively docile under Muslim rule until the early nineteenth century, when nationalist uprisings seeking linguistic as well as economic and political autonomy were set into motion by the First Serbian Insurrection of 1804. These uprisings were answered by the promise of Turkish reforms. Macedonian Christians began to demand a Macedonian clergy and Macedonian holy books and textbooks were written and even printed.

By the second half of the nineteenth century, Macedonian nationalists had begun to recognize the necessity for establishing a modern Macedonian literature, distinct from the Bulgarian and from the Serbian, as an indispensable element of Macedonian cultural identity. This recognition was engendered by the collection of Macedonian folk poetry and songs, a part of the setting down of the great oral record of Balkan history and tradition. Macedonian scholars such as Partenije Zografski and the Miladinov brothers, who published a collection of Macedonian songs in Zagreb in 1861 but perished in a Turkish prison in Istanbul for their efforts, provoked poets such as Rajko Žinzifov and Grigor Prličev to write the first modern poems in the Macedonian vernacular.

Although Turkish control over the region weakened, the Ottoman empire remained in control until 1912—in spite of an armed uprising in August of 1903 which resulted in the proclamation of a socialist Macedonian republic lasting only one week. But war drove the Turks from Macedonia in 1912, and for six years Macedonia was a battlefield. Peace would not come to the region until 1919; then the Peace of Paris divided the Macedonian lands. The southern coast was given to Greece, the Vardar valley to the new Kingdom of the Serbs, Croats, and Slovenes, the Pirin Mountains to Bulgaria. And the land—its villages ravaged, its fields despoiled, and many of its people departed—was devastated. It is no surprise that the Communist Party showed great strength there after World War I. When the Party was outlawed in 1920, Macedonia—in spite of Serbian efforts to repopulate the land and to pacify the people—became in parts a land without law.

With the coming of the Yugoslav state in 1929, repressive measures were undertaken in Macedonia to quell the banditry and social unrest. Macedonian students in Zagreb, in Belgrade, and in the new Macedonian philosophical faculty in Skopje joined student strikes. Macedonians had prominent roles in the rising tide of radical activity throughout Yugoslavia in the late 1930s.

The Thirties also saw the emergence of a period of intensified literary activity with writers such as the Realist poet-journalist Kočo Racin and Kole Nedelkovski, poet and imitator of folk songs. Both would die in the early months of the second World War in 1941, but their work established a beginning for the Macedonian poets who would follow.

The sudden capitulation of Yugoslavia in April of 1941 brought about a further partition of Macedonia, with Bulgarian fascists in the east and Italians and Albanians in the western regions. But a resistance movement, dominated first by Socialist nationalists and later by Tito's Partizans, almost immediately manifested itself. After the capitulation of Italy in 1943 German soldiers appeared in western Macedonia, but by then large areas were already under Partizan control. Skopje was liberated in November of 1944. Even during the fighting, however, Macedonian writers were quite deliberately producing poems and stories in a distinctly Macedonian language.

The post-war generation of Macedonian poets first produced a Socialist Realist poetry which celebrated the heroism of the Macedonian people's struggle against fascism and their triumphant movement toward nationhood. But before long many of these poets turned to more Modernist pursuits. Prominent in this generation was a young Partizan poet named Slavko Janevski. With the establishment on July 7, 1945 of the Macedonian language as the official language of the law courts and schools of the new Macedonian republic, which was by now one of six relatively autonomous republics that constituted

Tito's post-war Socialist Federated Republic of Yugoslavia, official recognition for what was at one time perhaps one of the most ancient and most recent of European literatures was finally achieved.

From the outset, the post-war Macedonian poets had two directions in which they might look. As Socialist Realists they could celebrate a post-revolutionary future; as Macedonians (especially after Tito's 1948 break with Stalin) they could reify their identity by looking into their past, not only to the literary nationalists of the nineteenth century but also to the Slavic people who stood beneath the walls at Salonika, who shared the glory of the Byzantines and the Nemanjids, who suffered under the Turks.

✦   ✦   ✦

Slavko Janevski, today one of Macedonia's most celebrated poets and novelists, looks in both directions. Born in 1920 in Skopje, Janevski attended technical school there before the war, then joined the Partizans and immediately became a presence in their world of writers and journalists. He wrote poetry during the war and published a collection *Krvava niza (Bloody Necklace*, 1945), one of the first collections of poems published in modern Macedonian. Other collections followed: *Pruga na mladosta (Railroad of Youth,* 1946), *Pesme* (Poems, 1947), *Egejski barutna bajka (The Aegean Gunpowder Plot,* 1950), and *Liriki (Lyrics,* 1951).

As one can see from even the earliest poems, those of the first section, Janevski's intent has always been lyrical. The poems almost always come back to singing, for Macedonians, in spite of the terrors of their history, have always sung. Sailors, bandits, monks, the peasants themselves—all sing, and their songs are not of words only. For singing makes words sound in a new way, in strangeness, beauty, and terror. It is of importance to poets interested in origins, poets like Janevski, to share in that singing.

Although in the early 1950s Janevski turned his attention to prose fiction and wrote *Selo za sedunite jaseni* (*The Village Behind the Seven Ash Trees*, 1952), he returned to publishing poetry in 1956 with *Leb i kamen* (*Bread and Stone*) and in 1966 published *Evangelje po star Pejo* (*The Gospel According to Old Peyo*), probably today his best-known collection. In these poems of the 1960s Janevski showed himself to be moving beyond the earlier work and in the direction of historical subject matter which had come to be of great interest among Yugoslav poets like Miodrag Pavlović and Veno Taufer. These new poems also displayed bold metaphorical experiments and established Janevski as one of Macedonia's most original and compelling, and indeed most difficult, Modernist poets. Another striking collection, *Kainavelija* (*The Tale of Cain*) appeared in 1968. Perhaps Janevski's most interesting and original poems are in these last two books—a selection from them is in the second section. The poems teem with strange creatures, reminiscent of Hieronymus Bosch, creatures composed of bits and pieces of men, animals and inanimate objects. ("The dagger opens its gills" is one example.) The presiding spirit of this imaginative generation is Sly Peyo, a trickster of a sensibility Americans can recognize from Indian tricksters' tales. Carl Jung spoke of the trickster as a "collective shadow figure," and certainly Peyo is such.

"It was light then, and yet it was dark," the Indian tale teller says. For Janevski as well, history is at base a creation myth, an account of the origins of the tribe. There was once a far time when earth and heaven, gods and men, were not yet separated, when all things were a part of all things, when all beings could change and make many different kinds of appearances. Once upon a time each part of the universe mirrored all others. It is this time which Janevski would seek. And he makes his search with the means of a trickster: "Sly Peyo dangles his legs from heaven's scythe." It is the exuberance of such imagery that raises our spirits.

The poems of the third section come mostly from a sequence entitled "Anatomija" ("Anatomy"). Here is to be found a different kind of mythmaking. Beginning in anatomical specifics, these poems probe, as it were, the psychic potential in each body part. Out of this process narratives are generated. Janevski is here an anthropologist of the anatomy, perhaps more aptly a necromancer of the body. In these poems he finds himself in the company of other twentieth century phenomenologist poets and fabulists—the Surrealists, Francis Ponge, and his own countryman, Vasko Popa.

—Milne Holton

The Bandit Wind

I

ПЕСНА НА ВЕЧНИОТ МОРНАР

Отидов по далечни друмја, јаболкницо, па сама ћутиш
срцето ми е кормилар слеп а бара заливи сини,
навечер ветар ли слушам пропаста ти ја слутам . . .
Дали неситост нечија коренот ти го кине
сам вака кога лутам.

Кога трипати в зори црно ќе писне косот
не чекај сонце. Слушај, јас уште друмови копам,
на јарбол црно знаме од крчма до крчма носам
и бол под теме кријам . .
О дали модри луњи ти носат модра пропаст
и дождја дали те бијат!

И веќе сили немам да дојдам смирен и висок
и чело да допрам на една заспана вода,
да одморам од удари раце на 'рж до сонце што пука
и пак во нигде одам . . .
Јаболкницо, есен е веќе, брег нема кај да се селам.
Те слутам сама и мала од една пуста лука.

THE SONG OF THE ETERNAL SAILOR

I went down an endless road; apple, you blossom alone.
My heart the blind helmsman who seeks the port.
If I hear the wind at dusk, I dream of your fall.
Is something tearing at your root
while I wander on alone.

When thrice at dawn the blackbird's shrill cry slit the darkness,
do not wait for the sun. Listen, hard roads I'm digging.
From one dive to another I carry a black banner on my spear,
and ache under my brow. . . .
O, does this blue moon foretell your blue fall,
and does the rain now beat you down?

I've no strength to come back tall, peaceful,
lean my forehead where water foams in its sleep,
rest my hands on the rye-stack as tall as the sun,
and then again take the road. . .
Apple, it's autumn already and no sight of land anywhere.
I dream of you half-grown and single in an empty port.

ТИШИНА

Кога булките ќе се истргнат од својот корен
и ќе појдат
една по една
кон својот залез
не следи ги
свадби веќе нема,
на секој чекор стои по една есен
смешна, бела и гола.

Кога булките ќе остават зад себе пустош
затвори го во себе дождот.
Нека ѕвони во олукот на твоите жили
под еден познат таван
И молчи.

Кога ќе падне ветрот на твојот прозор
со три писоци танки
и плач на незрел жерав
пак молчи.

Булките мразеа говор.

SILENCE

When poppies tear themselves away
from their roots
and start Indian file
toward the sunset,
don't go after them.
There are no more weddings.
At each step stands a single autumn,
foolish, white, and stark naked.

When poppies leave only waste behind,
shut up the rain within yourself.
Let it toll in the gutter of your veins
under the familiar ceiling,
and keep quiet.

When the wind alights on your window
with three high-pitched squeaks
and the sob of a young crane,
again keep quiet.

To poppies silence is golden.

БЕЗ ДНО

Се остава самиот себе како шара на килим. Сегде
низ градот. Афиш е на ѕидиштата. И уште
обивач со калауз моќен за многу врати во рајот
на заспаните жени. И стебло е в дрворед згуснат,
жилава кора за гладни ѕверки.
И ѕвер е со бело лице
под кожа со многу сачми.
И морнар без парче едро,
без кормило,
без гумен појас, без бог и ѓавол, морнар
за длабок асфалт, криумчар на љубовен отров.
И бусија зад секое ќоше:
му раснат нокти
и жили
и сабјести заби гладни до корен.
И оди. И плови. И чека. И – ништо:
ја нема . . .

Чуј, жено, те нема. Ноќва
тој апаш е. Аршин не нашол никој
за неговата мера.
Сите прозорски окна
и сите сенки зад нив
ги краде и ги крие во зениците свои
зад десет решетки црни –
те нема, те нема, те нема . . .

Во полноќ глув за петли и за крикоскок крвав
на една болничка кола и слеп
за Сатурн, за Уран, за една мала Венера
стои на плоштадот, влажен низ коски до земја,
и бара потсмев во нечии очи,
очи на случаен патник од крчма до последна база
и чека. Сиот е удар.

BOTTOMLESS

What he leaves in his wake resembles a pattern of some
    oriental carpet. Everywhere,
all over town is the poster on the wall,
the burglar with the mighty passkey
that opens doors in a heaven of sleeping women.
He's a tree-trunk in a thick row of trees
with tough bark for hungry animals.
He is the white-faced beast
with many pellets under his skin.
A sailor, too, without a bit of sail,
without a rudder,
without a lifebelt, without a god or devil,
a sailor for the asphalt pavements,
a smuggler of amorous poisons.
And the ambush behind every corner.
His nails grow,
and veins, and saber-shaped teeth,
hungry all the way down to their roots.
He walks. And floats. And waits. And nothing
happens. She won't come.

Listen, woman, you're late. Tonight
he's a street-corner hood.
No yardstick to take his measure.
Every windowpane and every shadow behind every windowpane,
he steals and hides in the pupils of his eyes
behind those ten steel-black bars —
you're late, you're late, you're late. . . .

At midnight, deaf to the roosters
and the bloody shriek of the ambulance,
blind to Saturn, Orion, and that little Venus,
he stands on the square, soaked through his bones
all the way down to the ground,
searching for a sneer in the eyes
of some chance traveler from this tavern to the very last one.
He waits, stricken.

7

Чекори патникот седнат и молчи.
Ги бара по земја сегде своите мртви очи.
Потсмев за него нема.
А тој – морнар без пристан –
витосан во вирје и витли
ја гризе нокта и стои
гризен од нокта и мелен.
Само по некоја сенка
кај да го допре, сегде
ќе остави модар белег.
Те нема, жено, те нема.

The bent-over passerby keeps quiet
as he looks for his dead eyes on the ground.
For him there's nothing to sneer about.
While he — a sailor without a port,
lost among puddles and whirlpools
gnaws at the night and the night
gnaws and chews him in return.
Wherever it happens to touch him,
it leaves a black and blue spot.
You're late, woman, so late.

МАЛА ТАЈНА

Да бидеш свој како што се свои водите
и тревите в небо загледани
да бидеш свој да бидеш свој како стеблата
да бидеш – како што е свој патот млечен
појди в гора кај е свое грлото на изворите
кај се свои гнездата на јасените
кај се свои капките крв што сме ги крстиле малини
и свои кај се лулките на пајаците
и на нив една осамена но своја капка роса
кај е свој разбојник еден палав ветар
кај е свој плачот на облаците
собран во врбовата зелена коса,

појди в гора, појди, појди сосем тихо
и собери ги тревите и крвта на малините
и испи ги изворите
и распори ги височините
и расфрлај го златниот прав на ѕвездите,
ќе никнат многу треви, води, птици со златни грла
ќе никнат бели птици, црвени птици, жолти птици
ќе слегне по нив сонцето со едно здраво
ќе дојдат по него девојките кришум
секоја ќе земе по една птица в дланка
од нив ќе напнат едра за едно море
покрив за една земја
стреа за една куќа.

Во морето излови ги бурите и полипите
и скроти ги
и спрегни ги да ја ораат земјата
и дојди под онаа стреа на таа една куќа
и крени ги рацете
и заиграј
и речи – девојки црни и бели и жолти,
девојки свој сум – речи.

SMALL SECRET

To be yourself the way waters are themselves,
and the grass that keeps staring at the heavens,
to be yourself to be yourself like the trees,
to be — the way the Milky Way is being itself —
to go into the woods where the spring's source is being itself,
where the nests in the ash trees are being themselves,
and the drops of blood which we call raspberries,
where the cradles of spiders are being themselves,
and in the cradles the lonely dew-drop,
where the wind, that mad bandit, is being itself,
where the weeping clouds are themselves
gathered in the willows' green tresses.

To go into the woods, to go, very quietly to go,
to gather grasses and the blood of raspberries,
and drink the springs dry,
and cut open the sky above
and spill the stars' golden dust.
Grass and water will grow, birds with a golden voice,
white birds will grow, red ones, yellow ones,
the sun will set behind them with a brief farewell,
after the sun the girls will come secretly,
each will take a bird in the palm of its hand
and will collect clouds and sunbeams
to make sails swell at sea,
to make a cover for the earth,
roof for a certain house.

Catch in the sea storms and octopuses
and tame them,
harness them to plow the earth,
then come under the roof of that house
and raise your hands,
dance
and tell — the black white and yellow girls —
girls I'm my own man — tell them.

11

СМЕАТА НА ОСАМЕНИОТ РАЗБОЈНИК

Би сакал како жена што се сака сè да имаш:
мојата песна разбојничка – висок, извиен повит –
бескрајна несовладлива зима бела,
моето грло по него со нокти да ровеш
и мојата девојка возбудлива како вино
како циганска песна и повеќе од неа врела.

И мојата тага би ја сакал – зар и неа? –
како мозаик оставена по безброј друмски крчми,
од момински срамлив залез до дива полноќ
и мојот волчи бес, волчи крик,
волче око сиво,
и моето чело по кое сенки играат болно
и мојата вечна глад и мојата вечна ситост
глад за живот и ситост од живот.

И моите другари (секој е од нив на бунт в срце ранет)
и нив би ги сакал со шумот на нивните жили
што секоја ноќ со гроздово млеко горат од занес,
тие сурови јаблани, банда по крв и било,
жилаво отровно горко месо за секој чакал –
и сè и сè што имам и сè што немам
ти сè би сакал.

Би ја сакал и мојата студена пештера пуста
тоа змиско гнездо
и мојата пченица како сачма тешка и густа
и мојата светлост, мојот мрак, моите ѕвезди
и сите стапки кои под модрата ничија стреа
и сите наши живи и сите наши мртви
и лулата што плови со дожд и бие со град,
и лулата би сакал да ја имаш, и неа.

LAUGHTER OF THE LONELY BANDIT

I desire, the way a woman is desired, for you to have everything:
my bandit's song like a tall, twisted ivy
and the endless white winter of my throat,
so that your nails may drill into it —
and that girl of mine as rousing as wine
or a gypsy tune, and still more passionate.

And my sorrow you'd want — oh that too!
left like a mosaic in countless taverns,
still shy at twilight, wild by midnight,
my wolf-like rage, wolf-like cry,
my grey eye of a wolf, my forehead
where shadows do their painful round dance,
my eternal hunger, endless satiety,
hunger rabid for life and my rich life,
and my friends (each with a wound of rebellion in his heart).
I want them now with the roar in their veins
that burn with the milk of the grape,
those rough poplars, that gang with bloody wrists,
that tough, poisonous, bitter meat that any jackal would feast on,
and everything else, everything I have and everything I have not.
I want that too.

I'd even want my cold empty cave,
that nest of vipers,
and my wheat, thick and heavy like buckshot,
and my light, my darkness, my stars,
and all my steps under nobody's blue eaves,
and all our living and all our dead,
and the storm that sails with rain and hits with hails,
that storm I want you to have and its victims.

И смеата на нашите деца тој водопад в пена
што шиба со илјади млазја и го разигрува денот
па со неа станува дете влажниот облак темен,
и оној љубовен шепот закопан кришум в сено
и сè што сум имал и имам и ќе имам
сè би сакал да ми земеш.

Би сакал. Па земи тогаш. И радост и црна мака.
На нишан затоа стојам со девет песни в заби
со вино в една со секира в друга рака.
Стрелај ме рамно в очи, таму е омразата моја,
омразата и мојата љубов гладна,
стрелај ме в грло крваво од песни и псости
и не чуди се што ни мртов нема да паднам.

And the laughter of our children, that waterfall
that with many torrents whips and livens up the day,
and the child, too, who becomes with it a part of a dark cloud,
and the lovers' whisper secretly buried in the haystack,
and everything that I had, and have, and will yet have.
I want you to take all that.

You want it. Take it then. All, every joy and suffering.
I stand in your gunsights with nine songs in my teeth,
in one hand I hold wine and in the other an ax.
Shoot straight in the eyes, that's where my hate is,
my hatred and my love yearning for passion.
Shoot into my throat bloody from songs and curses,
and don't be surprised if dead I remain standing.

II

СТАРИНСКИ ЗАПИС

По првата склавинска атака на
Тесалоники по суво и вода 616.

Туѓинци в жешки песоци лазат
бегаат нозе од луди глави
утроба гладна лисици пои
стапалки скокум секири газат
грклан со грклан в јазел се дави
господи чеда помилуј свои.

Смртта со магли полкови пои
летачки срца на меч се знаме
пропаски пијат од очи тага
од рамо рака скокум се двои
смачкани муцки џвакаат камен
господи скончај склавински враги.

В мраќава густа мракчиња коти
темница мајка и злото бабри
ноктеста чума Склавини дои
гниеж со ѕвезда в штама се плоти
на шии кама отвора жабри
господи чеда помилуј свои.

Крвави глави тикви со бради
зреат на мрсни крајморски ниви
плиснати очи полжавски траги
ќе мамат врани и сѐ ќе чади
од сончев оган по мугри сиви
господи скончај склавински враги.

18

Ancient Inscription

After the first Slav attack on Salonika in 616

Strangers creep over hot sands
feet run from the crazy head
hungry guts quench the thirst of foxes
bare soles leap from one ax-blade to another
larynx against larynx choking in a knot
forgive your children Lord

Out of fog's cauldrons death feeds the troops
the winged sword is an omen
the crows drink sadness out of the eyes
in flight the arm separates from the shoulder
shuttered jaws chew stone
make perish o Lord the Slav devils

In thick dark the dark drops another dark litter
mother dungeon keeps evil at bay
with its nails the Plague nurses Slavs
rot with stars quietly lies down
at the neck the dagger opens its gills
forgive your children Lord

Bloody heads like bearded pumpkins
ripen on the fat seacoast field
the trail of spilled snail-eyes
will lure crows in grey dawn
will fill with smoke from sun's own hearth
make perish o Lord the Slav devils

ЧАЛМА И КРУНА

Шејтан: жабешка глава
со жабри.
Светец: на петел јава
и бабри.

Две глави в игра
sунат.
Едната в чалма
другата в круна.

Чалма и круна. Крт и 'рт.
Добре ни дојде
дворјанко смрт.

Борач и пеливан
две глави скинати
се целиваат
обете зинати.

В носници веди
Заб до заб – топуз.
Нос чело боде.
Клепка гроб копа.

Две глави в шепот
зрееле. Пукаат.
Играат в слепота
очи си смукаат.

Од играчка плачка.
Сестричке палавичке

TURBAN AND CROWN

Devil with gills
and frog's head.
Saint riding a rooster
licked by flames.

Two heads in a game
toll.
One wears a turban,
the other a crown.

Turban and crown.
Mole and greyhound.
Welcome
sister death.

Wrestler and acrobat.
Two crushed heads
kiss each other, both
open-mouthed.

Lightning in the nostrils.
Tooth after a tooth — a mace.
A nose pierces a forehead.
Use an eyelash to dig a grave.

Two heads ripened
in a whisper, burst now,
play blinded.
Each other's eyes they suck.

Playing like that
one ends up crying.

сложно си играеме
премила главичке.

Од играчка
играчка.

Ќе си поиграме весело
очи лисици ни испиле
мозок куче побеснето.

Глава над глава
солза прокапала
глава на глава
уши излапала.

Сестричке главичке
дај ми крв земи крв
гвичке палавичке
тебе црв мене црв.

Безглави стави
бесстави глави
на едната царства земни
на другата небесни
на обете по едно царство.

На копуците окови претесни.

That game your toy.

Let's play gaily,
foxes have slurped our eyes,
rabid dogs our brains.

On top of a head another head
sheds a tear.
For another head some other head
ate the ears.

Sister head,
give or draw blood.
Crazy head,
you take one worm, I'll take the other.

Headless bodies, also
heads but without bodies.
To one kingdom on earth,
to the others a kingdom in heaven.
To everyone a kingdom.

And to the poor, tight chains.

КЛИМЕНТ

Едното око на другото
клепка му краде.

Меѓу себе забите се апат.

Ушите не се видуваат
да се зграпчат за уши.

Мозокот жедно себеси се пие.

Глава сум неглава.
Стоглавник без глава.

Громовите в љубов
јас труден со молни.

На луѓево чума јазик им цвака
јас онемувам.

Затоа на мојата лика зографска
оган седалка глобочи.

Секнатоно езеро
ми капе само од очи.

Па добро
очите ќе си ги ископам
за да прогледа слепилото.
Слушаш
очите.

CLIMENT

One eye steals an eyelash
from the other eye.

The teeth bite each other.

The ears hide
so they can't be pulling themselves.

The brain laps out of its own bowl.

I'm the head of the headless one,
hundred-headed and still headless.

Love-struck thunder
with lightning I impregnate.

Plague chews at everyone's tongue,
I'm struck dumb.

That's why on my icon-painter's face,
the fire deepens its seat.

A dried-up lake
drips out of my eyes.

Very well,
I'll scoop my eyes out
for my blindness to see better.

Do you hear that,
eyes.

ПЕСНА МОНАШКА ОД ЛЕШОК

Овде лежи Кирилово тело
у манастир у Лешок село
да Бог да за доброе дело

(Од Епитафот на Пејчиновиќ)

Зашто само јас ја знам таа жена.
На неа од машка мисла секое влакно е трудно.
Ту прилега на месо ту на ракиска пена.
Преку грб со префрлена боска петорки може да дои
сета од набожност и блудност.
Само јас ја знам од маките мои.

Но дојде ветрогонест крадец.
со биволска брада копито на маска очници од бигор
и крмачка грпка, дојде сам и гладен
со млеко жед рибја да пои.
Го видов в олтар дождалечки грбав
како ја граба од рацете мои.

И ја однесе в пламени магли в час кобен и суден.
По нив само моите раце појдоа жедни.
Главата се нурна в батак жив и студен.
На крстопат трупот остана да стои.

Апостоли бедни
молете се в присоиште за болките мои.
Зашто светец сум. В почивание. Гризам
и безглав само со срцето шупливо до корен
под укит на многулетна низа.

THE SONG OF THE MONKS FROM LESHOK

> Here lies Cyril's body
> in the monastery
> in the village of Leshok
> let good things come
> according to God's will

Only I know that woman,
so much she's desired
seems every one of her hairs is pregnant.
At times she's flesh and blood,
at times brandy foaming.
Pious and lewd with a tit over her shoulder
she can give suckle to quintuplets.
Only I know the troubles I have.

Then comes some idler some thief:
eye-teeth two stalactites,
hooves of a mule,
bison's beard and a hog's hump,
comes alone and hungry, thinks
milk will quench the thirst of fishes.
I saw him on the altar
arched like a salamander.
He grabs at my hands.

Fateful the hour when he took her into the flaming mist.
My thirsty fingers went after them.
The head stumbled into the living mud.
On the crossroads the body remained standing.

Miserable Apostles,
pray in the sunlight for all my pains to gather.
I am a saint. At rest. I gnaw even headless
with a heart hollowed out to its root,
under the hoar-frost of the year's rosary.

Векот од Адама смрт до смрт ми брои.
Ту Исус на дрво ту Нојо в море –
јас веќе немам соништа свои.
Оф леле таго добога.
хилендарско пострижение
ќе пијам ќе се напијам.
Дај ми нож да се прободам
по второто рождение.

Since Adam they count my deaths.
Once Jesus on the cross, once Noah in the sea —
I have no dreams of my own.
Ai! Sorrow all the way up to the almighty!
A monk, made in Mt. Athos.
Let me drink till I'm good and drunk.
Then give me a knife to kill myself
for some other birth.

ПЕСНА МУРАТОВА

По битката на Марица 1371

Роговита месечина боде
воден жител
видра икра мрести
в чест и причест
три петелски крести лисец на мраз пече
и ги толче в аван
јава триопашест шејтан згрбавен бог
козорог маторица опрасува
од модар дол
вол шестоног за селам се огласува
под змии свиен
пие мрак сончев зрак
со грб залепени близници се раѓаат
паѓаат и се распаѓаат камили на песок
тревите крај Марица пасат бели меса
под пајак се прпелка штука
гроб лулка смука
лулка гроб џвака
рака на рака крева тупаница
од скрка нокти прават ораница
едно око плаче
друго прска
по врска рајска саска молна-поскок
коско неисламска
коско варовна
коско бела
со два заба ќе те мелам
аскер земјава
трипати ќе ја обвитка со појас
на човечко грло гривест бегир појам.

THE SONG OF SULTAN MURAD

After the battle of Maritza, 1371

With its horns the moon pierces
the water creatures
the otter spawns its roe
in honor and in holy communion
the fox roasts over the frost three rooster combs
and pounds them in a mortar
a three-tailed devil rides a humpbacked god
the sow gives birth to a mountain goat
out of a blue valley
one hears a greeting of a six-legged bull
under the curled-up serpent
darkness drinks a ray of sunlight
Siamese twins are born
rotted camels fall in the sand
grasses by the river Maritza graze white meat
the pike squirms in the arms of a spider
the grave sucks the cradle
the cradle chews the grave
a hand raises a fist at another hand
out of the rocky soil fingernails make plowland
an eye cries
the other enlarges
on the ribbon of paradise the viper of lightning hisses
bone of infidels
rugged bone
white bone
with two teeth let me grind you
three times the soldier will gird the earth with his belt
while I water a black stallion
through a human throat.

БРАЌАТА СОЛУНСКИ

Ноќ. Скорпион влакнест.
Црн леплив и згмечен.
Ќелава мачко со влакнести шепи
земјата за опаш диво ја влече.
Ѕвезда за ѕвезда под уплав се лепи
близначки да се па јантари густи
паѓаат в стозаби кучешки усти
в утроби несити не ќе се светлост.
Јава на метлиште прчорог палав.
Молк. Не кикирига предзорник петел.
Сонцето гасне. Додека го жалат
киклопи-гуштери уши му лижат.
Трирога жаба се прпелка в пепел.
Илјади очи по магла се движат
слепи.

Невиделица. До Кирил и Методија.
Ќе биде што не било. За да биде биднината.
Било што не ќе биде. До нив.
Господи ќе има ли и по нив
слепи во иднината.

Браќата бради си палеле
бел оган да ги згрее
а вие не обвинувајте ги низ заби ѕвечави
што Некој—Си—Секој неплодно ги сеел
нивните букви во редови пелтечави.

BROTHERS FROM SALONIKA

Night. Shaggy scorpion,
black, sticky, badly beaten.
A bald cat with hairy paws
the earth pulls wildly by the tail.
Stars stick to one another in terror,
twins of dense amber
that fall into hundred teeth of a dog's mouth,
into hungry stomachs where they won't shine.
A crazy goat rides on a broom.
The early morning rooster doesn't crow. A deep hush.
The sun goes out. While it still burns,
cyclop-lizards lick its ears.
Three-horned frogs adhere to the ashes.
A thousand eyes rise out of the fog
blind.

Invisibility. All the way up to Cyril and Methodius.
There'll be what never was. Some future day to strengthen.
There was what'll never be. All the way up to them.
Lord, will the future have its blind
after these two saints?

They set their own beards on fire,
white fire to make them warm,
and you, don't blame them through your chattering teeth
because somebody-anybody fruitlessly sows
their words in stuttering rows.

ТИЕ УБИЈЦИ НА ЧОВЕКОВИОТ СПОКОЈ

Од икрите на покорот не ќе плисне сонот што те мачи.
Попусто виножитото змиски славолак плете.
Не чекам господарот на мракот повелба да ми врачи
за насмев што не бил ветен.

И нема кога ти велам прпелкав дождалец да сум.
Под оваа стврдната кожа гори скомињаво месо.
И ни крик ни скок ни протест колку и да сум касан.
Стојам. Од мраќава една потежок за капка блесок.
И така: патот ме носи очите кај што ме водат.
Остави ја својата примка за своја свечена кравата
Туѓа ми е да простиш лигурникавата ода
од просектурата во која песните се заклани јата.

Стојам. И стојам и чекам. Осуденик пред последен
                                                    чекор?
Никако. Морето мое со гусарски повик ме мами
во алги и корали во струи и нимфино млеко.
Добро е без вас да сум и вие без мене. Сами.

И стојам од веда до луња. И пловам од луња до веда
На српон небесен Пејо нозете си ги ниша.
Насмеан од Сатурн до Венера итрецот шашливо ме
                                                    гледа
и мисли самите и в магла капка безизлез ќе вдишат.

И се проѕева ѕјапач на Уран потпрен со теме
од каците на вековите до апатичност пијан.
Наеднаш далеку негде глув е за чекорот земен,
под перика на достоинство и ушите му се кријат.

Потоа? Никому ништо. Кон билјето на Андромеда
ќе појдам низ кристален сињак со хи-хи-хи-аксиома.
Во хаосот на редот по четврток доаѓа среда.
А тој кон што се стреми наеднаш до гуша тромав?

Those Killers of Our Piece of Mind

You won't get bad dreams by being a slave.
In vain the rainbow weaves its serpent-shaped triumphal arch.
I'm not waiting for the lord of darkness to present me
    with a charter
for the unexpected smile he encountered.

And I won't be, I'm telling you, a miserable salamander.
There's a flame of numb flesh under this hardened skin.
Neither a scream nor a leap nor a complaint — just something
    bitten by a whip.
I stand. Heavier than the darkness by an eye-beam.
And so. The road takes me where my eyes lead.
Let the noose be your holiday necktie.
Forgive me, sugary odes are foreign to me
when they rise from the dissecting rooms of slaughtered flocks.

I stand. The condemned one about to take his last step. I stand
    and wait.
No one. My sea calls me with its pirate's call
into algae and coral, into currents, milk of nymphs.
It's good that I'm without you and that you are without me. Alone.
Standing between the lightning and the storm. Sailing from
    the storm back to the lighting.
Trickster Peyo dangles his legs from the heaven's scythe.
Grinning from Saturn to Venus the sly one hunts me in his
    cross-eyed way
while fog-bound thoughts breathe in drops of hopeless mud.

Leaning the back of his head on Orion, the idler extends his yawn.
From the diddle-daddle of centuries to their indifference he
    drinks a toast.
Somewhere far, deaf to his earth-bound footsteps, he sings
and hides his ears under the wig of pride.

And then. It doesn't matter. Towards the herbs of Andromeda
with my ha-ha for axiom I'll set out across the crystal hoar-frost.
In that chaos's rule, Thursday gives birth to Wednesday.
Toward what goal, then, does he now strain, heavy-assed?

ИТАР ПЕЈО ЗА ЕДЕН ДРУГ

Место епитаф

Вепарски заби, секач и дерач,
пуздрава моја со рез ја мерат.

Сум сакал. Мразам. Мразејќи сакам.
Бедра ми лапа брадолик чакал.

Жед сон ми пие. Прав жеден пијам.
Сок сладок в жили ми розга змија.

Сабја ме стрела. Стрела ме сече.
Сонувам небо. Земја ме влече.

Кажи ми земјо, вселенска мравко,
каква е трошка Јаневски Славко.

Кажи ми што е: роб или владар.
И дали пее в скрб кога страда.

И што е – злодеј судија закон?
И што е што е? Глаголи мако . . . .

Ене го. Мини пеколни зема.
Под срце мина. Над глава свеќа.

Бил. Не е. Збогум. Веќе го нема.
Веќе го нема

веќе го
веќе . . .

Од сите страни вдовици в црно
на гроб му носат вино и цвеќе.

Суша е.
Солзи затоа врнат.

SLY PEYO TALKS ABOUT SOMETHING ELSE

In place of an epitaph

Wild boar's teeth cut and rip,
my weak flesh they measure.

I loved. Now I hate. Hating, I love.
With my thighs the jackal eased his hunger.

Thirst drinks my dream. I drink dust.
What sweet juice the rattler squirts into my veins.

The saber slays. The arrow cuts down.
I dream of heaven. The earth has me entangled.

Tell me, O earth, you cosmic ant,
what kind of crumb is Slavko Janevski?

Tell me, is he a slave or a king?
Does he sing while he suffers in pain?

Is he an outlaw, or the judge, or the law itself?
What exactly is he? Say it slowly, suffering....

There he is. Readying his infernal machine.
A mine field under his heart. Candles above his head.

He was. No, he wasn't. Farewell. He's gone.
Already gone. Already...

From every side mourning widows
bring flowers and wine jugs to his grave.

There's a drought.
That's why the tear-drops are falling.

III

НАЈПРВИН НОЖ

И најпрвин бездруго да ги отчепиме
непознатите пештери на милениумите
за да дојдеме преку коски и заблуди до себеси
виличави до чекорот последен и потаму
да се видиме меѓу дренки и оскоруши
ние глутница над пресно мечешко месо
додека во каделите на бизонските бради
ни чаделе светулки и палеолитски скарабеи
и гаснеле очи под сенка на каменен чекан
но пред тоа да појдеме од јама на уплав
кон соништата пред светлоста на првата песна
и да се видиме како презреани паѓаме од ветки
врз папра (на жените да им е помеко под нас)
и да се видиме во врутоци сури
меѓу полноглавци со кои сме лекувале глад и поштук
додека скомињави искушенија нè мамеле
кон злобништва од кои челата ни сјаеле црвено,
да се погледнеме тогашни и да се послушаме
додека со воздишки чинари од карпи сме корнеле
Богови кога ќе ни подарите огнови
од бронза или од незнамшто да го исковаме ножот
човекољубиво во предиграта да си поиграме
и да му го забуцаме на братот меѓу плешки
да жугне како 'ркулец од златнорујни клобурци
првата песна за дивите афиони.

Такви да се видиме и да се чуеме —
слушате ли, Каинавеловци?

First the Knife

To begin with we must open
the unknown caves of the millennium
to reach ourselves over the bones of error
jabbering to the very end and then further
to appear among cornelian cherries and service trees
like a pack over fresh bear meat
while in the curls of our bison-like beards
crickets and paleolithic scarabs smoke
and our eyes turn dim in the shadow of a stone mallet
but before that let's quit these terrifying pits
toward dreams before daybreak and in the first song
see ourselves falling ripe off the branches
on the ferns (for the women to have it soft as they lie under us)
and to see in the brutal currents
among tadpoles whose hunger and madness we keep curing
while teeth-numbing temptations lure   us
toward prophecies of doom from which our foreheads
     glow red-hot
for us to see each other by and listen to what we formerly were
while with heavy sighs we ripped maples out of rocks —
Gods, when will you make us a gift of fire
so that out of bronze or something else we may hammer a knife
magnanimously to play with it first
then stick it between our brother's shoulder blades
make it sprout like a seed out of reddish bubbles
this first song to the wild poppies.

To see and hear ourselves just like that —
are you listening, you of Cain's clan?

СРЦЕ

Сочувај ја легендата за него.

Тоа патува со ветерни мелници.

Натопи го со оган на намери
назобај го со искушенија
скрши го на две како бела погача.

Едната половина закопај ја со првата љубов
другата во кафез од магли затвори ја.

Птицо речи и птицо
исплачи ми ги празниве гради
а самиот исклешти се.

Те убедувам –
во празнината на ребрата
поудобно ќе се смести твојата сенка.

По светов премногу сенки лазат.

HEART

Preserve its legend.

It travels with windmills.

Soak it with the fire of ambitions,
let it peck among temptations,
break it in half like a loaf of white round bread.

Bury one half with your first love,
lock the other in a cage of fogs.

Say to it bird, bird,
mourn my empty breast —
and as for yourself — just laugh.

I'm about to convince you —
your shadow will inhabit
this empty cage more comfortably.

Too many shadows already crawl over this earth.

ЈАЗИК

Кога главата ќе ти се стркала
под дното на животот
и устата ќе се отвори
за нечујна воздишка
јазикот умно се подава
да ѝ ги излиже раните на земјата.

Со свој мелем дрвјата ги лекува
со свој мов каменот за топлина го обвива
со своја благост соленото море го смирува.

Како појас континентите ги обвива.

Кога ќе се наскита
се враќа кон своите корења
обогатен со мудроста на вечната смиреност
за да помолчи
на хебрејски
на ерменски
или на македонски.

Сеедно, љубов моја,
на сите јазици јазикот еднакво молчи.

Така и молчењето си го премолчува.

Tongue

When your head slides down
to that bottom-life,
and your mouth opens
for the inaudible sigh,
the tongue wisely sticks out
to lick the earth's wounds.

With salve to heal the trees,
with its moss to swaddle the stone in warmth,
with its gentleness to make the salty sea calm down.

Like a belt girding the continents.

When it has had enough of wandering,
it returns to its root
grown wise in eternal repose
to keep silent a little
in Hebrew
in Armenian
in Macedonian.

It doesn't matter, my love,
in every language the tongue is silent,

and thus, can't say nothing of its silence.

КРВ

Нејзината жед се вика споулавеност.

Кога е жедна си го пие изворот.
Пијана светот го поплавува.

На секој чекор стапици постава.
Од отпор до отпор на бесилка те носи.
Од кол до кол на кол те наденува.

Најтемно ѝ е бездруго
кога в крчма се разденува
кога името ѝ е жед, љубов моја,
кога името ѝ е Безименост.

И кога од секоја нејзина капка
ќе плисне по еден крвоскок пенест
(најпрвин надвиснат над бездните на свеста
потоа урнат од ураган силен)
сети се, љубов моја ненаспана,
дека еднаш и ние сме биле.

И присокри една капка на чување.
Нашето догледање е веќе збогум.

Збогум, љубов моја, без простување.

BLOOD

Her thirst is called madness.

Thirsty she drinks at her own source.
Drunk, she floods the world.

Sets traps at each and every step.
From one uprising to the other,
She carries you to the gallows,
From pole to pole too, to impale you.

How dark she must turn
At the day's breaking in a tavern,
When thirst is her name, my love,
When her name is the Nameless One,

And when out of her every drop
Blood fizzes, blood spews forth
(Lifted first beyond the mind's abyss,
Then thrown down with a strength of a storm).

Remember my insomnia, love
Those times when we were alive,
And hide and guard one drop to the end.
Our "till we meet" is already a "farewell."

Say farewell, my love, without leave-taking.

РАЦЕ

Едната на земјата утробата ѝ ја корне.
Другата небото за брада го влече.

Кога ја месат иднината
до раменици во жилавост се даваат.

Но погледни ги кога ќе се скараат.
Левата со нокти жилите на десната ѝ ги скубе.
Десната со жили ноктите на левата ѝ ги шиба.
Ако се склопат во набожна школка
дланките меѓу себе се излапуваат.

Во творештвото, господи,
твоја се лика-прилика
кога изгризани
мелем во раните си дуваат.

Безрак, раскажи им еднаш на планините
за десетте плуски на рацете таткови
војувачи в рудници
и копачи во војните.

HANDS

One plucks the earth's innards,
the other pulls at heaven's beard.

When it's the future they knead,
shoulder-deep they drown in gristle.

Or look at them when they fight.
The left scratches the veins of the right one,
the right one uses its veins to whip the nails back.
Even when they gather in the shape of a pious seashell,
inwardly the palms devour each other.

When they're making something, Lord,
they're your spit-image.
When bitten
they blow on their wounds.

Amputee, tell them about the mountains,
about ten callouses on the hands of ancestors,
those soldiers in mines,
ditch-diggers in wars.

ОЧИ

Се извртуваат љубопитни.
Сакаат во себе да ѕирнат
на свој извор со солзи да се искапат.
Попусто им е, љубов моја, попусто.
Изворот со сокрвца се оклопил.

Сега со клепки по многуте тајни копаат
и бараат да им се раскаже
прикаска за слепилото.

И така темницата на копје им е кренета.
Течат. Ќе претечат. Зашто ни ги испиле
светлопадите на сите вселени.

Потоа во глобовите ќе им прилегнат
грутки иловица под сув босилек,
бели китки под твоите солзи.

EYES

They turn curiously
Wanting to peek into themselves,
to bathe at the source of their tears.
In vain, my love, in vain.
Dried pus covers their source.

Now their lids veil over secrets
and ask to be told
the story of blindness.

And so darkness lifts them on a spear.
They ooze and will cease to ooze
since they haven't drunk enough of
that cosmic lightfall.

Then, in their pits, there they will lie,
under dry basil and lumps of clay,
the white bouquets of your tears.

ПАУНИЦА

Под крилото носи ден
на клунот капка песна
в очи недоречен сон . . .

Четири пауни со крик се кинеа
па прскаше од нив љубов и крв.

Четири –
а кога брестот се наведна над нив
виде црвена река
и мртви крилја
и очи за љубов гладни.

Под крилото сега носи мрак
на клунот глад и јад
в очи неречена милост.

Птицо, боли ли да имаш љубов –
љубов и мртво крило?

Peacock

Under her wing she carries daylight,
in her beak a drop of song,
in her eyes an unfinished dream.

Four peacocks slit each other with a cry;
blood and lust rushed out of them.

Four —
and when the elm tree bent over them,
they saw the red river,
the dead wings
and eyes thirsty for love.

Under her wing she carries darkness,
in her beak hunger and bile,
in her eyes undeclared tenderness.

Bird, does it hurt to carry love —
love and a dead wing?

СКАМЕНЕТИОТ ОРФЕЈ

Сонцето заспива на врв бескрајно стебло
Со глава е в бездна.
Со срце в камен.
Сенката му е вжештено злато.

А тој исчекува. Орфеј.
Сиот е од дабови жили
и од тајни
и од зломолклив лишај
Лежи како карпа меѓу карпи
со левата дланка врз нечие срце
со десната во сржта земна
со обете пред тоа
врз харфата на мртвите души.

На грбникот му заспала змија.
Крик е. Ветар во ветар.
Евридико круно на моево чело
проѕирен простору на празново срце
бескрају на крајов мој вечен
беспатицо во длабока јама
до кога смртта твоја
мој вечен живот ќе е.

Во челуста чеканот на времето
му ја крши утехата на чекањето.
Попусто сонцето со нишки го обрабува
и со цветни ѕвона му ја раскажува венчавката
на она што било и она што не ќе е.

ORPHEUS TURNED TO STONE

He imagines the sun at the top of an endless spear.
His head in an abyss,
heart inside a stone,
his shadow a gold leaf.

He waits. Orpheus.
Made up of secrets, oak-veins,
ill-tempered moss. Lies
like a stone among stones
with left hand on someone's heart,
the right in the earth's marrow,
and the two of them together
on harp of dead souls.

On his backbone a viper dozes.
And the scream. Wind inside a wind.
Eurydice, crown from my forehead,
transparent space of my empty heart,
endlessness to my own end,
open space to my own deep pit,
how long will your death
give me eternal life?

In the jaws time's hammer
shatters the consolation of waiting.
Uselessly the sun frames him with its threads
while with its golden bell it tells of a wedding between
what was and what will never be.

Бог е на самотијата.
Осаменик меѓу боговите.
Песната од која и небото оглувнува
се вика тишина
се вика празнина
се вика горчина.

Само од длабочина
во која ни мракот на сее мракава
плете свои плетенки понорна река
и се одѕива безгласно
Евридика Евридика Евридика.

Само водата.
Таа.

God of solitude,
solitary among gods.
His song drowns out the heavens.
Silence is summoned,
emptiness is summoned,
bitterness. Only
out of depths
where even the dark won't sow darkness,
the sunken river braids its hair
and voicelessly echoes
Eurydice Eurydice Eurydice

Only water.
Taa.

Notes

THE SONG OF THE ETERNAL SAILOR
Jabuka (apple) is a term of endearment in Macedonian, as *chou* (cabbage) in French.

ANCIENT INSCRIPTION
In the sixth century A.D. the Byzantine fortress at Salonika was repeatedly assaulted by the Slav tribes, newly settled in the Macedonian lands. They never succeeded in taking the fortress, but the attacks unified the Slavic tribes.

BROTHERS FROM SALONIKA
Two monks from Salonika, Constantine (Cyril) and his brother, Methodius, were sent in the ninth century as apostles to Greater Moravia. They formulated the "Cyrillic" (and/or perhaps the Glagolithic) alphabet to aid them in their work. These were the first alphabets for the Slavic languages.

CLIMENT
Above the lake and the medieval theological center which is today the city of Ohrid stands the Church of Our Most Glorious Lady (Crkva Bogorica Perivlepta), the home of one of the most valued collections of Orthodox icons in the world. One of the treasures of this collection is a highly stylized iconographic portrait of St. Climent, a disciple of Cyril and Methodius and first bishop at Ohrid from 870 to 893 A.D. Climent was also among the first to establish a literature in the Church Slavonic. Together with his successor, St. Naum, he founded the literary school of Ohrid.

The references to blindness here are an allusion to the peasant (or Muslim) habit of defacing the eyes in frescoes and icons in the Macedonian churches. They may also allude to the tradition which tells us that upon the defeat of the forces of the Bulgarian Czar Samuil by the Byzantine forces of Basil II at Mt. Belarica in 1014 A.D., fifteen thousand of the captured Bulgarian soldiers were blinded and returned to their emperor at Ohrid.

THE SONG OF SULTAN MURAD

Murad, the great military commander of the Ottoman Turks, led their armies in the bloody battle against the Serbian and Macedonian princes at the River Maritza in 1371, won there a famous victory, and established the Turkish presence in Macedonia for six hundred years. In 1389 Murad again led the Moslem Turks against the Christian forces at the Battle of Kosovo. Murad was killed by Milos Obilic in this battle. Again Kosovo was traditionally seen as a Turkish victory, for afterwards Turkish control of the Balkans was assured.

THE SONG OF THE MONKS FROM LESHOK

Near the monastery of Sv. Bogorodica (St. Mary) in the village of Leshok, an ancient Macedonian village near Tetovo in western Macedonia, is the grave of Cyril Pejcinović, an Orthodox monk and literary figure of the first half of the nineteenth century (d. 1845). Pejcinović was one of the first to write in the Macedonian vernacular.

THOSE KILLERS OF OUR PIECE OF MIND

In 1966 Janevski published a set of poems with the crafty "Star Peyo" ("Peyo the Sly") as his peasant *persona*.

About the translator and general editor

CHARLES SIMIC was born in Belgrade in 1938 and came to United States with his family as a child. For his poetry and translations he has won awards from the American Academy of Arts and Literature and has received the Edgar Allan Poe Award and the PEN Translation Prize. In 1990 he was awarded the Pulitzer Prize for poetry for *The World Doesn't End* and has recently published his tenth book of poetry, *The Book of Gods and Devils*. A distinguished translator, he has translated work of Vasko Popa, collected in *The Little Box* and in *Homage to the Lame Wolf*, Ivan V. Lalic, collected in *Fire Gardens*, and other Yugoslavian poets in *Four Yugoslav Poets*. A 1984-1985 MacArthur Fellow, Mr. Simic is currently Professor of English at the University of New Hampshire; he lives in Strafford, New Hampshire with his wife and two children.

MILNE HOLTON is the author recently of *Cylinder of Vision: The Fiction and Journalistic Writings of Steven Crane*. A professor of English Literature at the University of Maryland, College Park, he is the editor of *Reading the Ashes: An Anthology of the Poetry of Macedonia* and *The Big Horse and Other Stories of Modern Macedonia*. He has co edited (with Vasa D. Mihailovich) *Serbian Poetry from the Beginnings to the Present: An Historical Anthology*, (with Herbert Kuhner) *Austrian Poetry Today*, and (with Paul Vangilisti) *The New Polish Poetry*.